CONTENTS

HEAVILY ARMOURED

The oddest-looking dinosaurs were often covered with armour – horns on their faces, spines and plates down their backs, and bony clubs on their tails.

The first dinosaurs were small and fast-moving. They had no armour because they could escape quickly from their predators. Over time, larger, heavier dinosaurs appeared. These creatures moved slowly and were vunerable to attack by predators. Their bodies were armoured to make it difficult for predators to kill them.

The first armoured dinosaur was *Scelidosaurus,* from the Early Jurassic Period. It had armour plates made from knobs of bone that grew in the skin, just like the thick scales of a crocodile today. Later, dinosaurs with unusual head features appeared. These included the 'bone-heads' or the pachycephalosaurs, the 'horn-faced' ceratopsians, and the long-snouted hadrosaurs or duckbills.

Pachycephalosaurs
A dinosaur with a skull roof.

Ceratopsian
An armoured dinosaur with horns on its face.

Stegosaurs
This dinosaur had plates and spines on its back and tail.

DISCOVERING DINOSAURS
WEIRD & WONDERFUL

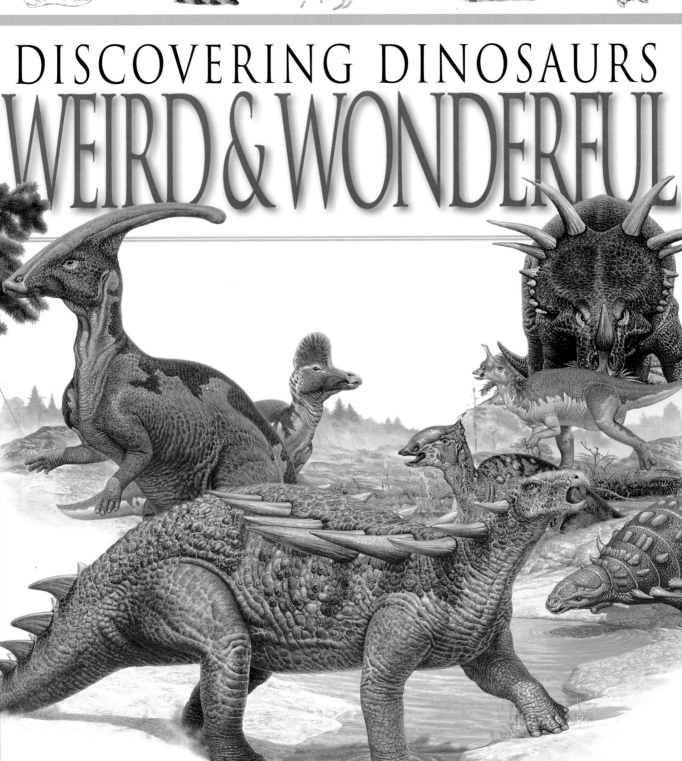

MICHAEL BENTON

© 2015 Alligator Publishing Limited

Author: Prof. Michael Benton BSc, PhD
Illustrator: John Sibbick

Published by Alligator Publishing Limited
2nd Floor, 314 Regents Park Road
London N3 2JX
England

Printed in China 0259

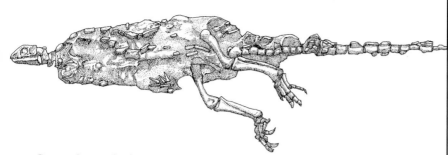

Complete skeleton
Scelidosaurus *was first discovered in England in the 1850s. Bone plates were found around the skeleton. In the 1990s, some armour plates were also found in Arizona, USA.*

Tail
Scelidosaurus *had a strong tail lined with armour spines.*

ankle bones

hoof-like claws

Broad feet
Scelidosaurus *had stumpy feet. The finger and toe bones ended with small hooves instead of proper claws.*

Back
Scelidosaurus *had rows of bony plates down its back.*

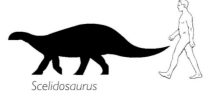

Scelidosaurus

HOW DO I SAY THAT?

⦿ **CERATOPSIAN**
SER-AH-<u>TOP</u>-SEE-AN
⦿ **HADROSAUR**
<u>HAD</u>-ROH-<u>SAWR</u>
⦿ **PACHYCEPHALOSAUR**
<u>PACK</u>-EE-<u>KEF</u>-AL-OH-<u>SAWR</u>
⦿ **SCELIDOSAURUS**
SKEL-<u>ID</u>-OH-<u>SAW</u>-RUS
⦿ **STEGOSAUR**
<u>STEG</u>-OH-<u>SAWR</u>

DINOSAUR DEFENCES

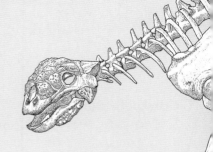

Armour was a great defence for plant-eating dinosaurs. They could not run fast, so they just stood their ground when meat-eating dinosaurs attacked them. The ceratopsians had horns on their faces, which made for deadly weapons. *Centrosaurus* had a large nose horn that pointed forwards. When it was faced by a hungry *Tyrannosaurus rex*, *Centrosaurus* could scare it away by swinging its head from side to side. If the predator got too close, it would lunge with the horn. One blow could result in a fatal wound.

The ankylosaurs had rows of bony plates covering their bodies. These plates were locked together like chain mail. When attacked, an ankylosaur like *Nodosaurus* or *Polacanthus* may have crouched over its tail and legs, making it impossible for a predator to sink its teeth into the ankylosaur's body. Ankylosaurs were huge and hard to budge. This made it difficult for a predator to kick the ankylosaur over to get at its fleshy belly.

DINO DICTIONARY

- **Ankylosaur:** an armoured dinosaur
- **Ceratopsian:** a 'horn-faced' dinosaur
- **Predator:** a meat-eater

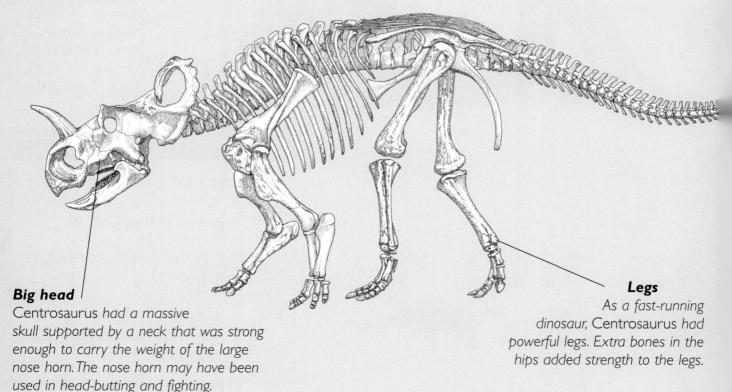

Big head
Centrosaurus had a massive skull supported by a neck that was strong enough to carry the weight of the large nose horn. The nose horn may have been used in head-butting and fighting.

Legs
As a fast-running dinosaur, Centrosaurus had powerful legs. Extra bones in the hips added strength to the legs.

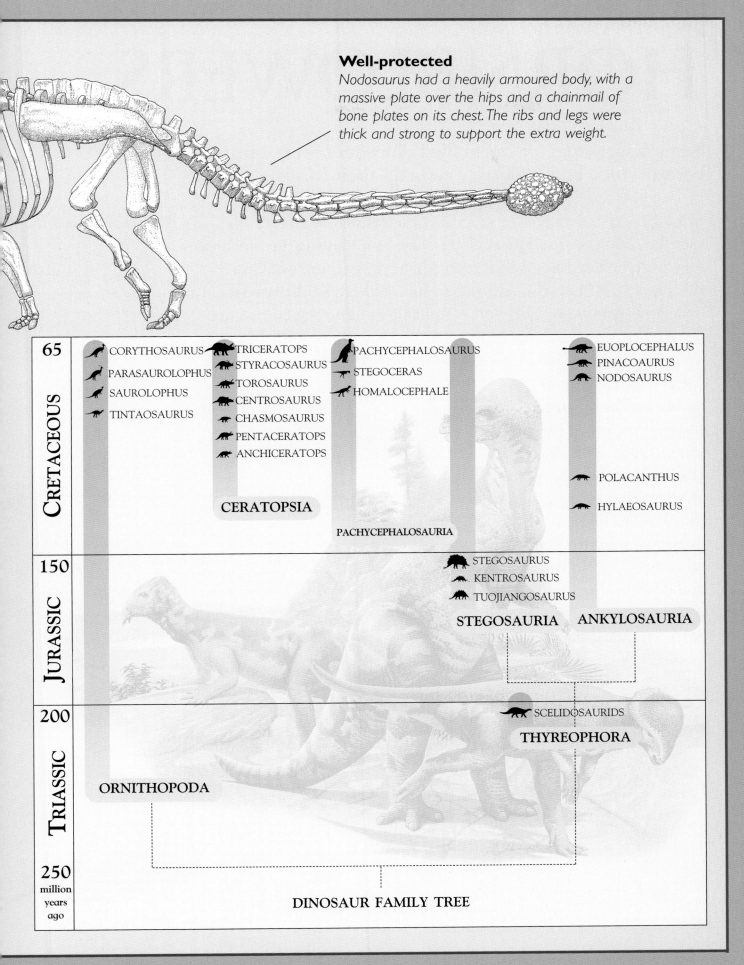

Well-protected

Nodosaurus had a heavily armoured body, with a massive plate over the hips and a chainmail of bone plates on its chest. The ribs and legs were thick and strong to support the extra weight.

65				
	CORYTHOSAURUS	TRICERATOPS	PACHYCEPHALOSAURUS	EUOPLOCEPHALUS
	PARASAUROLOPHUS	STYRACOSAURUS	STEGOCERAS	PINACOAURUS
	SAUROLOPHUS	TOROSAURUS	HOMALOCEPHALE	NODOSAURUS
	TINTAOSAURUS	CENTROSAURUS		
		CHASMOSAURUS		
		PENTACERATOPS		
		ANCHICERATOPS		

CRETACEOUS

CERATOPSIA

POLACANTHUS

HYLAEOSAURUS

PACHYCEPHALOSAURIA

150	STEGOSAURUS
	KENTROSAURUS
	TUOJIANGOSAURUS

JURASSIC

STEGOSAURIA   **ANKYLOSAURIA**

200	SCELIDOSAURIDS

THYREOPHORA

ORNITHOPODA

250
million
years
ago

TRIASSIC

DINOSAUR FAMILY TREE

HORNBLOWERS

Some hadrosaurs, or duckbilled dinosaurs, were unusual because they had fantastic crests on their heads.

Scientists have debated for years why hadrosaurs had crests on their heads. Some thought they were used for fighting, but because they were hollow, they would probably have been too weak for this purpose. Others thought the crests could have been used as underwater snorkels. This, too, is unlikely because the crests have no opening for breathing. Most scientists now think that the crests were used for signalling and calling to other dinosaurs in the herd.

Each species (kind) of hadrosaur had a unique crest shaped that made its own sound. Male sounds were different to female sounds. Scientists have made models of the tubes inside the crests to find out what the dinosaurs sounded like. The tubes ran up from the nostrils and down to the throat. When a hadrosaur breathed, the air passed through the crest and made a honking noise.

Tsintaosaurus
The short, tubular crest that pointed forwards on the forehead was unusual. Most crests pointed backwards.

Saurolophus
A crestless dinosaur with a strange point at the back of its head. Its nasal passages opened into a broad area on top of the snout, which was probably covered with loose skin. The dinosaur could blow up the skin like a balloon and let out a great bellow.

HOW DO I SAY THAT?

● **CORYTHOSAURUS**
KOR-<u>ITH</u>-OH-<u>SAW</u>-US

● **PARASAUROLOPHUS**
<u>PAR</u>-AH-<u>SAWR</u>-OR-<u>LOAF</u>-US

● **SAUROLOPHUS**
<u>SAWR</u>-OH-<u>LOAF</u>-US

● **TSINTAOSAURUS**
<u>CHING</u>-DOW-<u>SAW</u>-RUS

1. Tsintaosaurus 2. Saurolophus
3. Corythosaurus 4. Parasaurolophus

Parasaurolophus

In addition to a long tube at the back of its head, Parasaurolophus may have had a sail of skin between the crest and the neck. This sail may have been brightly coloured and acted as a signalling device.

Corythosaurus

This dinosaur had a crest shaped like half a dinner plate. Breathing tubes run around inside the crest like the tubes of a French horn.

FACTFILE: CORYTHOSAURUS

Lived: 90-70 million years ago

Group: Ornithopoda

Size: 10 m long

Weight: 5 tonnes

Discovery: 1914, Alberta, Canada

Diet: Herbivore

Special features: plate-like head crest

Name means: 'Corinthian helmet reptile'

ORNITHOPODS

Different hadrosaurs may have had very different head features, but their skeletons were almost exactly the same. These dinosaurs were big animals, weighing between five and ten tonnes, but they were very common. At some sites in Mongolia and North America, hundreds of skeletons are found preserved together. Hadrosaurs walked slowly and fed while standing on all four feet. To run at speed, they lifted themselves up on to their back legs. Their long tails stuck out straight behind and helped to balance the body.

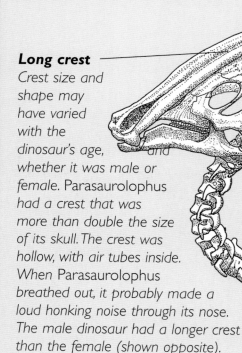

Long crest
Crest size and shape may have varied with the dinosaur's age, and whether it was male or female. Parasaurolophus had a crest that was more than double the size of its skull. The crest was hollow, with air tubes inside. When Parasaurolophus breathed out, it probably made a loud honking noise through its nose. The male dinosaur had a longer crest than the female (shown opposite).

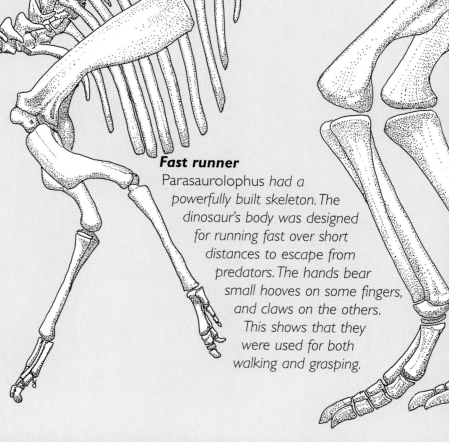

Fast runner
Parasaurolophus had a powerfully built skeleton. The dinosaur's body was designed for running fast over short distances to escape from predators. The hands bear small hooves on some fingers, and claws on the others. This shows that they were used for both walking and grasping.

THE ORNITHOPODS:
- *Corythosaurus*
- *Parasaurolophus*
- *Saurolophus*
- *Tsintaosaurus*

Cross-section of duckbill shaped-heads

Some scientists believe that the crestless duckbill dinosaurs may have had inflatable skin flaps that stretched over their broad snouts.

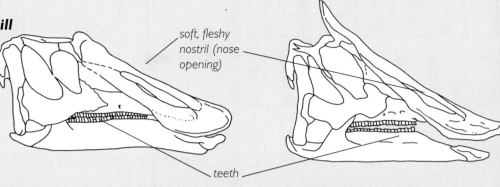

soft, fleshy nostril (nose opening)

teeth

Prosaurolophus *skull*

Sauralophus *skull*

Strong back

Hadrosaurs had a mesh of bony rods along their backbones, which gave them extra strength.

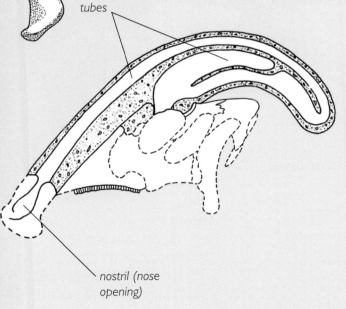

hollow nasal tubes

nostril (nose opening)

DINO DICTIONARY

● **Skeleton:** the bony framework that supports the body

● **Skull:** the bones of the head

Female head

This cross-section shows the tubes inside the bony crest of a female Parasaurolophus. When the animal breathed, air passed through the nostrils, up one side of the crest, down the other and then into the throat. There was no hole at the top of the crest, so it could not have been used as a snorkel as scientists once believed. Other hadrosaurs had similar systems of breathing tubes inside their crests.

HORNED GIANTS

Many ceratopsians had horns on the nose and face, as well as a bony shield to protect the neck.

Ceratopsians lived in the Late Cretaceous Period. Large numbers of fossil skeletons have been found in the same place, so these dinosaurs probably lived in big herds. Ceratopsians may look fierce, but they were in fact plant-eaters. They had many small teeth that could chop through plant stems and other tough vegetation.

The most famous ceratopsian is *Triceratops*. It had a classic ceratopsian nose horn, which was similar to the horn of a rhinoceros. It also had two larger horns – one over each eye. If *Triceratops* lowered its head and faced its deadly enemy, *Tyrannosaurus rex*, it would have been hard for the predator to attack without getting badly hurt. *Centrosaurus*, a close relative of *Triceratops*, had one huge single horn on its nose and two smaller horns curling over its neck shield or frill.

Mouth
*Like all ceratopsians,
Triceratops had a horn-covered,
toothless beak. This was used for
snipping off mouthfuls of plant food.*

FACTFILE: TRICERATOPS

- Lived: 75-65 million years ago
- Group: Ceratopsia
- Size: 9 m long
- Weight: 6 tonnes
- Discovery: 1887, Colorado, USA
- Diet: Herbivore
- Special features: three horns, neck frill
- Name means: 'three-horned face'

1. *Centrosaurus*
2. *Triceratops*

2

1

⬤ **CENTROSAURUS**
SEN-TRO-<u>SAW</u>-RUS
⬤ **TRICERATOPS**
TRY-<u>SER</u>-AH-<u>TOPS</u>

WHERE DID THEY LIVE?

⬤ *Centrosaurus* ⬤ *Triceratops*

Neck shield

At the back of the head of Triceratops was a long neck shield made of bone and covered with skin. The edge was lined with diamond-shaped bony studs. This giant frill protected the dinosaur's fleshy neck from attack by predators.

Spikes and curls

Centrosaurus had a neck shield formed from a broad rim of bone surrounding two big holes. These holes were probably filled with muscle and covered with skin. The back edge of the neck shield was lined with small spikes. Curling over the top were two sharp horns.

LONG-FRILLED DINOSAURS

Some dinosaurs not only had vicious face horns, but also long heads with huge neck shields, known as frills.

The massive neck frills and horns of ceratopsians must have been heavy to carry around. So why did they have them? It is likely that they were used for defence against *Tyrannosaurus rex* and the other huge predators of the Late Cretaceous Period. Male ceratopsians during fights with each other might have used their heads as weapons. Perhaps they locked horns like male deer do today, and wrestled with each other until one gave in.

   Some scientists believe that the frill was an area of bone for that held the jaw muscles. It may be that the frills were brightly coloured and used for signalling to other members of the herd.

1. *Chasmosaurus* 2. *Anchiceratops*
3. *Pentaceratops* 4. *Torosaurus*

WHERE DID THEY LIVE?

● Anchiceratops and Chasmosaurus
● Pentaceratops ● Torosaurus

Chasmosaurus
A dinosaur with a short nose horn, as well as a horn above each eye. The long neck frill was square and edged with spikes. This head-on view is what Tyrannosaurus rex *would have been faced with as it tried to attack!*

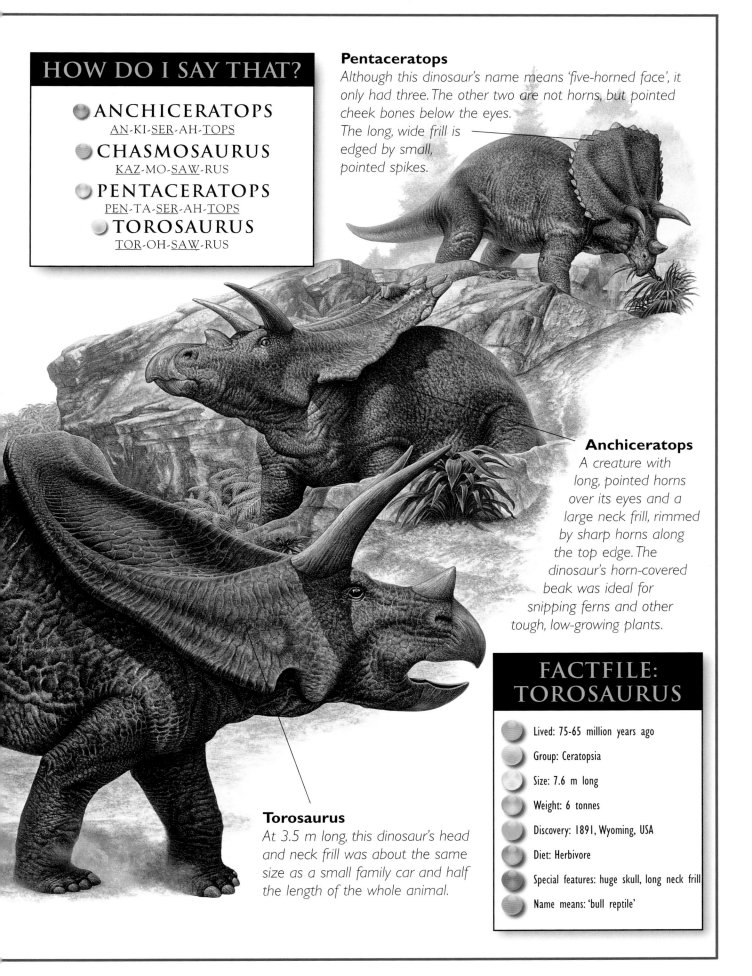

HOW DO I SAY THAT?

● **ANCHICERATOPS**
AN-KI-SER-AH-TOPS

● **CHASMOSAURUS**
KAZ-MO-SAW-RUS

● **PENTACERATOPS**
PEN-TA-SER-AH-TOPS

● **TOROSAURUS**
TOR-OH-SAW-RUS

Pentaceratops

Although this dinosaur's name means 'five-horned face', it only had three. The other two are not horns, but pointed cheek bones below the eyes. The long, wide frill is edged by small, pointed spikes.

Anchiceratops

A creature with long, pointed horns over its eyes and a large neck frill, rimmed by sharp horns along the top edge. The dinosaur's horn-covered beak was ideal for snipping ferns and other tough, low-growing plants.

Torosaurus

At 3.5 m long, this dinosaur's head and neck frill was about the same size as a small family car and half the length of the whole animal.

FACTFILE: TOROSAURUS

● Lived: 75-65 million years ago

● Group: Ceratopsia

● Size: 7.6 m long

● Weight: 6 tonnes

● Discovery: 1891, Wyoming, USA

● Diet: Herbivore

● Special features: huge skull, long neck frill

● Name means: 'bull reptile'

CERATOPSIA

The ceratopsian skeleton was strong because these dinosaurs needed powerful arms and legs to support their huge weight. The most unusual features of these dinosaurs are their nose horns and neck frills. Most ceratopsians weighed more than a modern elephant, so they were unable to run very fast. When attacked by a carnivore, the main defence of the ceratopsians would have been to stand firm and present their horns and neck shield. The ceratopsian's skull presented a tough wall of bone and horn. Even *Tyrannosaurus rex* would have thought twice about trying to leap at a ceratopsian from the front, since the horns would have caused a bad wound.

As herbivores, ceratopsians probably lived the way cows do today – cropping and chewing plant food all day. The horn-covered beak snipped off plants and the tooth-lined jaws ground up the plant material. The food then passed down into a huge stomach housed inside the rib cage.

THE CERATOPSIA:
- *Anchiceratops*
- *Centrosaurus*
- *Chasmosaurus*
- *Pentaceratops*
- *Protoceratops*
- *Torosaurus*
- *Triceratops*

Big head
All ceratopsians had similar skeletons, but each species had a different arrangement of horns and frill. This Chasmosaurus skeleton shows the huge head in relation to the body.

Limbs
The bones of the arms and legs were stout and pillar-like, just like a modern elephant. A ceratopsian may have looked a bit like a rhinoceros, but it was four or five times bigger.

DINO DICTIONARY

- **Carnivore:** an animal that feeds on meat

- **Herbivore:** an animal that feeds on plants

Defence tactics

A herd of ceratopsians may have defended itself from attack by forming a circle around its young. By facing outwards with their neck shields lowered and horns pointing straight out, they would have been a tough challenge for predators, such as Tyrannosaurus rex.

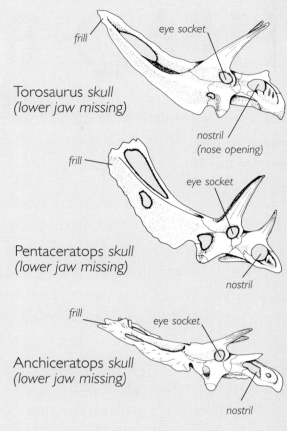

frill   eye socket

Torosaurus *skull (lower jaw missing)*

nostril (nose opening)

frill   eye socket

Pentaceratops *skull (lower jaw missing)*

nostril

frill   eye socket

Anchiceratops *skull (lower jaw missing)*

nostril

Skull shapes

These pictures of ceratopsian skulls show how the lengths of the nose and forehead horns vary between dinosaurs. The bony frill had holes in it to save on weight. If the frill had been solid, the dinosaur's head would have been too heavy to lift off the ground!

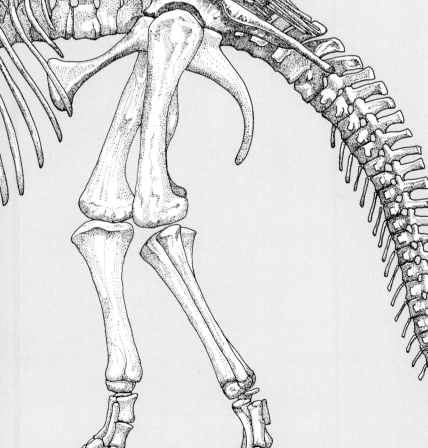

HEAD-BUTTERS

Pachycephalosaurs were an odd group of dinosaurs, with their dome-shaped heads and bird-like feet.

The fossilised teeth of a pachycephalosaur were first found in the 1850s, but scientists were unable to work out what they were. Then, in 1924, a skull and skeleton of *Stegoceras* were discovered. *Stegoceras* was a small, two-legged, plant-eating dinosaur, similar to an ornithopod. But unlike ornithopods, it that had a head as strong as a safety helmet. Scientists called this dinosaur a pachycephalosaur.

Why did the pachycephalosaurs have such thick skulls? One of the largest pachycephalosaur was *Pachycephalosaurus*. All its skull bones were of normal thickness for a dinosaur. But the roof bones were 22 centimetres thick. The domed head was also rimmed by bony knobs. Pachycephalosaurs may have head-butted each other in fighting rituals, where males tried to win females. The thicker the skull, the more successful the male would be in a contest.

HOW DO I SAY THAT?

- **HOMALOCEPHALE**
  HOM-AL-OH-KEF-AL-EE
- **PACHYCEPHALOSAURUS**
  PAK-EE-KEF-AL-OH-SAW-RUS
- **STEGOCERAS**
  STEG-O-SER-AS

Homalocephale
A 'flat-headed' dinosaur with a lower skull roof than most other pachycephalosaurs.

WHERE DID THEY LIVE?

Homalocephale
Pachycephalosaurus   Stegoceras

Pachycephalosaurus
The biggest pachycephalosaur was eight metres long. Only its skull and a few fragments of the skeleton have been found. The thick skulls are more easily preserved as fossils than the other parts of their skeletons. The body of Pachycephalosaurus shown here is based on fossil finds of other, smaller pachycephalosaurs.

1. Stegoceras 2. Homalocephale 3. Pachycephalosaurus

FACTFILE: STEGOCERAS

Lived: 80-70 million years ago

Group: Pachycephalosauria

Size: 2 m long

Weight: 50 kg

Discovery: 1902, Alberta, Canada

Diet: Herbivore

Special features: thick skull roof, bony frill

Name means: 'horny roof'

Stegoceras
*The body shape
of this well-known
pachycephalosaur
is based on several
skeleton finds. Skeletons
of Stegoceras show that
the skull roof grew thicker
as the dinosaur grew older.*

PACHYCEPHALOSAURIDS

Pachycephalosaurs had light skeletons compared to their thick skulls. The teeth were quite small, which means that pachycephalosaurs must have fed on soft plants. As with the ornithopods, pachycephalosaurs had long, slender legs. This would have made them good two-legged runners. It is likely that their main defence from the meat-eaters was speed.

A pachycephalosaur involved in a head-butting contest would have charged forwards very quickly – its backbone level and head lowered. As the two animals crashed heads, the force of the blow would have run through the skull and down the neck, producing a loud cracking sound. This would have shaken the brains of these dinosaurs. But they had such small brains, that it probably did not matter much!

Neck bones
Not much is known about the bones in the neck of Stegoceras. Scientists believe that they must have been especially strong to absorb some of the energy of the impact when skulls crashed together during fights.

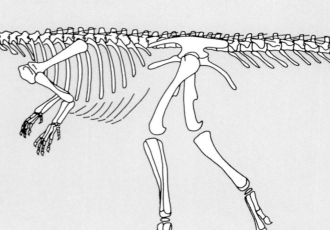

Head
In the head-butting position, the backbone was held straight as the pachycephalosaur ran at the speed of a racehorse. The top of the skull was rounded so that the impact of the blow would be hardest in the centre. The heads of two head-butters in contest would face towards the side.

Grasping hands
Stegoceras *had five digits on each hand. These would have been useful for grasping and grabbing bunches of leaves.*

DINO DICTIONARY

● **Paleontologist:** a person who studies fossils

Head-cracking fun

Scientists imagine that the clash of heads sent out loud bangs that could be heard at great distances away. Today, mountain goats and bighorn sheep crash heads in a similar way during fights.

THE PACHYCEPHALOSAURIDS:

- *Homalocephale*
- *Pachycephalosaurus*
- *Stegoceras*

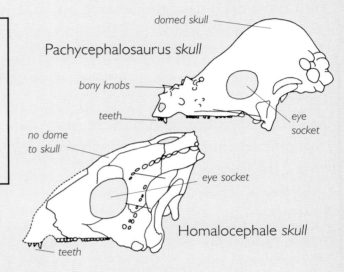

Pachycephalosaurus *skull*

domed skull

bony knobs

teeth

eye socket

no dome to skull

eye socket

teeth

Homalocephale *skull*

Stegoceras

Not much is known about the skeleton of Stegoceras. Many of the features (faded elements shown here) have been reconstructed using skeletons of other pachycephalosaurs.

Skull shapes

Heads of pachycephalosaurs varied in shape. Some, such as the head of Pachycephalosaurus, were completely rounded. Others, such as Homalocephale, were lower and sloped up to a point at the back. All the pachycephalosaurs had bony knobs and hornlets on their snouts and around the edges of the thickened skull roof. This edging is like the frill at the back of a ceratopsian skull. It suggests that these dinosuar groups were probably close relatives.

PLATED BEASTS

With its spiky tail and double row of plates running down its back, *Stegosaurus* is one of the best-known dinosaurs.

The huge bony plates that ran down the backs of these dinosaurs may not have been used for defence, since they did not offer much protection. Some scientists think that the plates may have been used to control body temperature. Fossil evidence suggests that the plates may have been covered with skin and a network of blood vessels. On a cool morning, *Stegosaurus* may have stood sideways, with its plates facing the Sun, and absorbed heat through the skin and blood vessels. If the dinosaur became too hot, it would then turn away from the Sun to cool down.

The tail spikes were almost certainly used as weapons against attack. By swinging its tail, *Stegosaurus* could give its main enemy, *Allosaurus*, a dangerous blow that could rip the predator's belly open.

Tuojiangosaurus
At six metres long, this dinosaur was smaller than Stegosaurus. It had smaller plates that were spaced like a fence along its back. The tail spikes were similar in shape to the cone-shaped back plates.

Kentrosaurus
This was the smallest stegosaur – only two-and-half metres long. It had narrow plates and spikes down its back. These may have also covered its hips and shoulders, which may have provided extra defence.

Small head
This view of Stegosaurus shows how tiny the dinosaur's head was, compared to its broad back and plates.

1. Stegosaurus 2. Tuojiangosaurus 3. Kentrosaurus

Stegosaurus
Since they were not fixed to the skeleton, it is hard to know exactly how the plates appeared on the body of Stegosaurus. It is likely that the plates were arranged in a double row on the back with a slight overlap between each plate.

WHERE DID THEY LIVE?

Kentrosaurus

Stegosaurus   Tuojiangosaurus

HOW DO I SAY THAT?

KENTROSAURUS
KEN-TRO-SAW-RUS

STEGOSAURUS
STEG-OH-SAW-RUS

TUOJIANGOSAURUS
TOO-OH-JEE-ANG-OH-SAW-RUS

23

STEGOSAURIDS

Stegosaurs had huge arms and legs to support their weight. The broad backbone and ribs carried the heavy back plates and spines. This meant that a stegosaur was not built for speed. The arms were half the length of the legs, making it hard for the stegosaur to run without tipping up on its nose. The dinosaur's head also seems very small compared to the rest of its bulky body.

Dinosaurs had relatively small brains for animals of their size. This is why most scientists think they were not very intelligent. *Stegosaurus* is considered to have been an unintelligent dinosaur. For an animal weighing more than the largest living elephant, *Stegosaurus* had a tiny brain – about the size of a walnut. If you compare this to mammals today, the brain of *Stegosaurus* was the right size for a kitten!

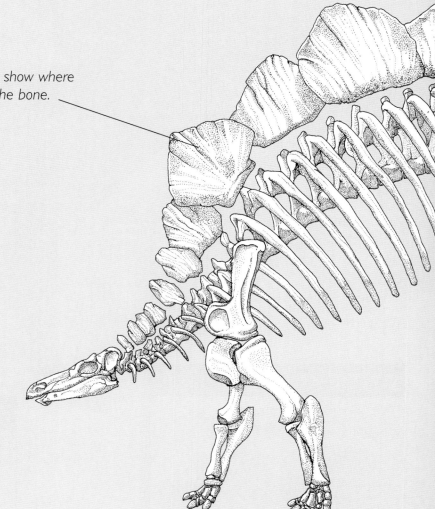

Plates
The patterns of ridges and channels show where the skin and blood vessels lay over the bone.

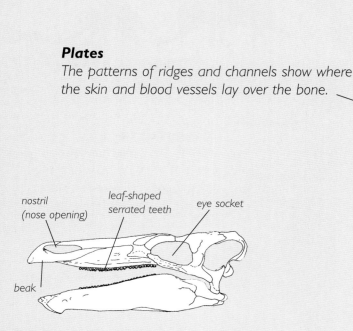

nostril
(nose opening)

leaf-shaped
serrated teeth

eye socket

beak

Head
The narrow skull of Stegosaurus had a tiny space for the brain at the back. The front of the mouth did not contain teeth, and was probably covered with a horny beak for snipping off plants. The small back teeth were used to chop up soft plants.

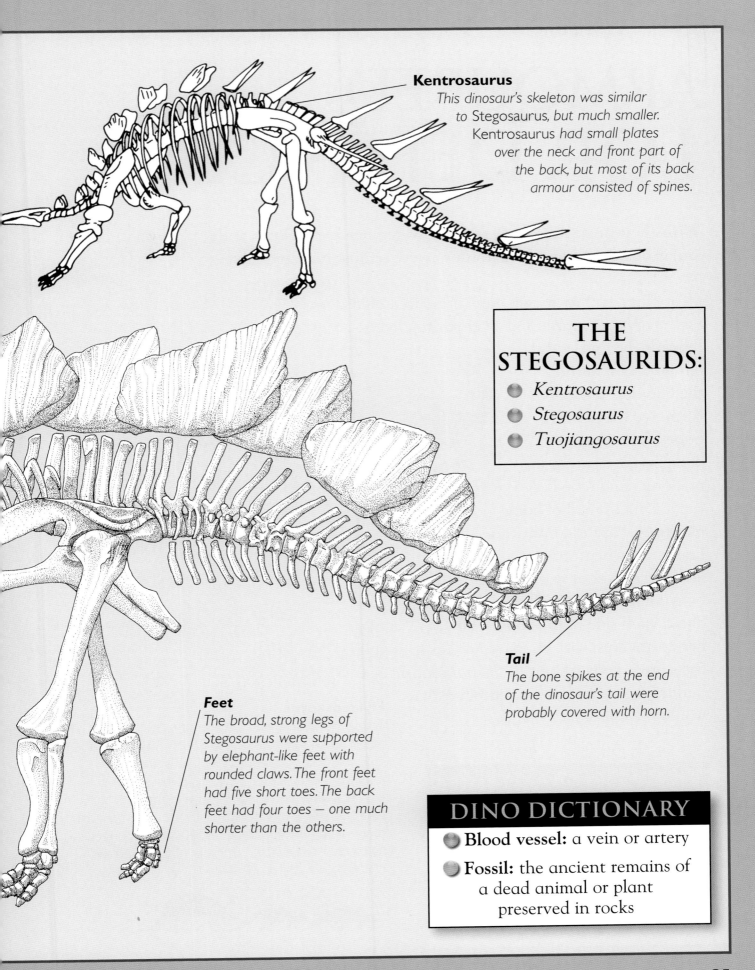

Kentrosaurus
This dinosaur's skeleton was similar to Stegosaurus, but much smaller. Kentrosaurus had small plates over the neck and front part of the back, but most of its back armour consisted of spines.

THE STEGOSAURIDS:
- Kentrosaurus
- Stegosaurus
- Tuojiangosaurus

Tail
The bone spikes at the end of the dinosaur's tail were probably covered with horn.

Feet
The broad, strong legs of Stegosaurus were supported by elephant-like feet with rounded claws. The front feet had five short toes. The back feet had four toes – one much shorter than the others.

DINO DICTIONARY
- **Blood vessel:** a vein or artery
- **Fossil:** the ancient remains of a dead animal or plant preserved in rocks

ARMOURED FOR DEFENCE

With their protective body armour of regular bony plates and larger pieces of bone, ankylosaurs were almost indestructible.

Most plant-eating, four-footed, armoured dinosaurs, such as *Hylaeosaurus* and *Nodosaurus,* lived towards the end of the dinosaur age during the Cretaceous Period. They needed to be armed for defence against meat-eating predators and relied on a rugged chain mail of bony plates. Nodosaurid ankylosaurs had narrow heads, pointed tails and leathery skin that was studded with bony lumps. Some had rows of long spikes along each side of the body. They were stocky, heavy animals, with short, stout legs to support their great body weight. If *Tyrannosaurus rex* had tried to attack these dinosaurs, it would have broken its teeth.

HOW DO I SAY THAT?

🔵 **HYLAEOSAURUS**
HIGH-LEE-OH-SAW-RUS

🔵 **NODOSAURUS**
NODE-OH-SAW-RUS

🔵 **POLACANTHUS**
POLE-AH-KAN-THUS

Hylaeosaurus
The third dinosaur ever discovered was named Hylaeosaurus in 1833. Only the front part of this creature is known from fossil evidence. Protective armour is obvious — the neck, body and tail were covered by rings of tough chain mail, made up of small bony plates that locked together. Larger bone knobs ran in rows down the middle of the dinosaur's back and rows of long, sturdy spikes along each side of its body.

1. Hylaeosaurus 2. Polacanthus 3. Nodosaurus

Nodosaurus

This large dinosaur did not have spikes, but its well-organised body armour was just as tough. Even fearsome T. rex would not have been strong enough to break through the tightly locked, squarish plates that covered its back. Nodosaurus came from North America and would not have lived with the other dinosaurs shown here.

FACTFILE: HYLAEOSAURUS

Lived: 1130-115 million years ago

Group: Ankylosauria

Size: 4 m long

Weight: 1 tonne

Discovery: 1833, England

Diet: Herbivore

Special features: bony armour, spikes

Name means: 'woodland reptile'

WHERE DID THEY LIVE?

Hylaeosaurus and Polacanthus

Nodosaurus

Polacanthus

As with Hylaeosaurus, fossil skeletons of Polacanthus are incomplete. The tough armour plates and spines can survive in rocks where softer bones have been lost.

CLUB-TAILED DINOSAURS

Some ankylosaurs not only had complete body armour but also giant bony clubs at the ends of their tails.

Measuring some six metres long, and weighing up to three tonnes, ankylosaurs such as *Euoplocephalus*, were like huge tanks. When these imposing creatures were attacked, they would crouch down towards the ground and rely on their invincible armour to protect themselves from predators. Their clubbed tails were strong and could make accurate blows when defence was required.

As herbivores (plant-eaters), ankylosaurs had small, leaf-shaped teeth and horny beaks. Mostly, they swallowed their food whole. Plant food is difficult to digest, which is why ankylosaurs had barrel-like bodies and enormous stomachs. Imagine the rumblings, grumblings and explosions after an ankylosaur had eaten its lunch!

Euoplocephalus
This dinosaur had an extra layer of bony plates on top of the skull bones. The four spines around the back of the head provided extra protection even the eyelids had a bony cover.

1. Pinacosaurus 2. Euoplocephalus

HOW DO I SAY THAT?

⬤ **EUOPLOCEPHALUS**
YOO-<u>OP</u>-LO-<u>KEF</u>-AL-US

⬤ **PINACOSAURUS**
<u>PIN</u>-AK-OH-<u>SAW</u>-RUS

FACTFILE: EUOPLOCEPHALUS

Lived: 80-70 million years ago

Group: Ankylosauria

Size: 6 m long

Weight: 2 tonnes

Discovery: 1902, Alberta, Canada

Diet: Herbivore

Special features: armour spikes, tail club

Name means: 'true plated head'

Pinacosaurus

A dinosaur with an armoured knobbly skull, and dense armour plates over its neck, back and tail. The dinosaur's tail club was huge. It was made of bone that was fixed to the backbone at the end of the tail. This was a fearsome weapon that could have knocked any predator senseless.

WHERE DID THEY LIVE?

Euoplocephalus Pinacosaurus

ANKYLOSAURS

UP CLOSE

An ankylosaur skeleton was designed to support the huge weight of the armour. The bony plates and spines provided great protection, so these dinosaurs did not need to run fast to escape from predators. Ankylosaur arms and legs were short and pillar-like, just like those of an elephant today. The ribs and backbone were strong to carry the armour and the large stomach. The small head was protected by rock-hard armour. The tail had strong muscles running down each side, and the ankylosaur could swing its tail club with enough force to kill a predator.

Rock solid
When attacked, Hylaeosaurus probably defended itself by crouching down, tucking its arms and legs under its body, and waiting for the predator to go away. The armour plates and the spikes on the sides of the body prevented the predator from getting at any fleshy part of the body.

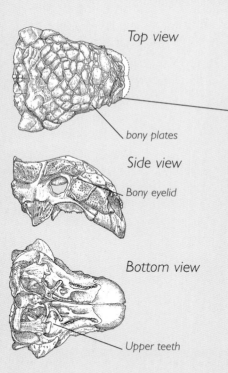

Top view

bony plates

Side view

Bony eyelid

Bottom view

Upper teeth

Skull
Different views of an ankylosaur skull show the extra layers of thick, bony armour. A mosaic of small bones covered the normal skull bones. Each ankylosaur species had a different pattern of skull armour. The bony eyelid and the tiny teeth can also be seen in the side view and bottom view.

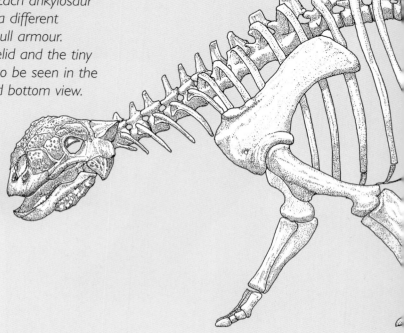

DINO DICTIONARY

⬤ **Girdle:** a bony arch to which an arm or leg is attached

⬤ **Vertebra:** one of the bones that make up the backbone

THE ANKYLOSAURS:

- *Euoplocephalus*
- *Hylaeosaurus*
- *Nodosaurus*
- *Pinacosaurus*
- *Polacanthus*

Tail clubs

The tail end of Ankylosaurus was made up of two bony knobs or plates that formed in the skin. These were fused to either side of the vertebrae in the tail.

Top view

Bottom view

Side view

Powerful weapon

The ankylosaurids protected themselves by giving meat-eating dinosaurs a mighty whack with their massive tail clubs. A well-aimed blow to the head could easily have killed a predatory dinosaur such as T. rex.

Euoplocephalus skeleton

The strong shoulder and hip girdles were designed to stand up to huge forces. The hip bones were strengthened because they were fixed to seven or eight joined vertebrae, forming a wall. This partly supported the weight of the body armour, but it also provided attachments for the tail muscles.

Top view of Euoplocephalus

This picture shows the broad hip bones needed to support the heavy armour.

INDEX